YELLOWSTONE

Ruth Kirk

YELLOWSTONE
The First National Park

Photographs by Ruth and Louis Kirk

A MARGARET K. MC ELDERRY BOOK

Atheneum 1974 New York

Photographs by Ruth and Louis Kirk, Bob and Ira Spring, The Washington State Historical Society and from the National Park Service. (Unless otherwise credited, the photographs are by Ruth and Louis Kirk.)

Map by Bernhard Wagner

Copyright © 1974 by Ruth Kirk

All rights reserved

Library of Congress catalog card number 74-76273

ISBN 0-689-50006-8

Published simultaneously in Canada by McClelland & Stewart, Ltd.

Manufactured in the United States of America by

Halliday Lithograph Corporation

West Hanover, Massachusetts

First Edition

Contents

YELLOWSTONE

YELLOWSTONE NATIONAL PARK

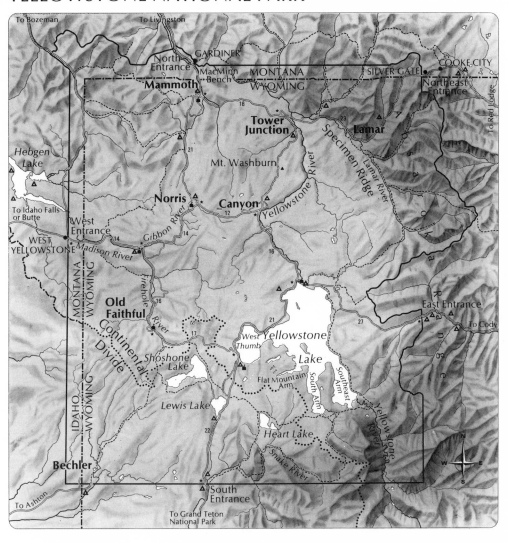

To Bozeman   To Livingston

North Entrance   GARDINER
Mammoth   MacMinn Bench   MONTANA
WYOMING   SILVER GATE   COOKE CITY
Northeast Entrance

Tower Junction   Lamar
18   29

Mt. Washburn   Specimen Ridge   Tamar River

Hebgen Lake   21   Yellowstone River

To Idaho Falls or Butte   Norris   Canyon
West Entrance   12
WEST YELLOWSTONE   14   Gibbon River   14   16
Madison River
MONTANA   Firehole River
WYOMING   16
Old Faithful   21   27   East Entrance
Continental Divide   17   West Thumb   Yellowstone   To Cody
Shoshone Lake   Lake
Flat Mountain Arm   South Arm   Southeast Arm
IDAHO   Lewis Lake   Yellowstone River
WYOMING
22   Heart Lake
Bechler   Snake River

N
South Entrance   W   E
To Ashton   S
To Grand Teton National Park

MONTANA

IDAHO

WYOMING

△ Campground
♦ Visitor Center
── Road
------ Trail
★ 16 ★ Mileage

0   5   10   15   20 MILES

A geyser steams like smoke from a campfire alongside the Firehole River. Wisps of steam rise as underground heat reaches the surface. Elk by the thousands graze the park's meadows.

The Land

YELLOWSTONE NATIONAL PARK IS NATURE WITH ALL THE pieces still in place. Geysers steam and spout like smoke from a thousand campfires, and springs of hot mud boil and bubble. Woodpeckers hammer the trunks of lodgepole pines and elk graze in emerald meadows. Moose wade in marshes and ponds, plunging their heads to the bottom to feed on aquatic plants, while ducks dabble at the surface close by. Buffalo and bighorn sheep, deer, antelope, bears, coyotes, even wolves roam free, their lives following the rhythm of the seasons.

Man belongs in this wilderness too, but he comes to look and enjoy, not to change the land. No cities. No farms. No golf courses or zoos. This national park is the biggest in the United States outside of Alaska, and the oldest anywhere in the world. It stretches for 3,000 square miles across the central Rocky Mountains. Peaks stand as high as 13,000 feet and even vast rolling plains average 6,000 or 7,000 feet in elevation. The lowest valley lies more than a mile above the level of the ocean.

The Yellowstone region straddles the Continental Divide. Some of its rivers drain to the Atlantic, some to the Pacific, and one pond actually drains in both directions. This is Isa Lake, quiet and small, cradled in a grassy fold right on the divide. Yellow water lilies float on its surface and water-strider insects dart about like skaters at a rink. Nothing looks special, yet whenever rain or melting snow fills Isa Lake to overflowing, the strange drainage takes place.

One end empties into a creek that starts for the Missouri and Mississippi rivers. By this route, Yellowstone water belongs to a system flowing into the Atlantic Ocean. The other end of the lake empties in the opposite direction. Its overflow eventually joins the Snake River, which flows into the Columbia. The Columbia, in turn, empties into the Pacific.

Summer rainstorms pound so hard in Yellowstone that a car's roof sounds like a drum and windshield wipers can't keep the glass clear. Or sometimes summer storms bring snow instead of rain, and campers wake up to a white world even in July or August. White tent, white trees, white ground—all because of wet, soft, summer snow.

Often, wind howls across the land, occasionally gusting ferociously. "I've had St. Elmo's fire in my hair during a thunderstorm and have been knocked across the room when lightning hit the phone line while I was making a call," a lookout wrote in his report describing summer work on a fire tower. "But wind can be the most frightening of all. There's so little you can do about it.

"Today a storm hit suddenly. The wind jumped from 30 miles per hour to 60 and must have been gusting into the 90s. The door flew open and everything—books, papers, pans, blankets—suddenly began tumbling about and getting drenched. The windows bulged like they were made of Saran

A three-toed woodpecker rests in its nest hole.
Water from Isa Lake drains to both east and west.

Each winter, huge icicles sheath the lip of Yellowstone Falls.

Wrap and the catwalk was too slippery to stand on. All I could do was build a fortress out of furniture, then sit in the middle and hope it would protect me against flying glass if the windows broke. It took two hours for the clouds to dump their load and the wind to spend its force. I've been twice that long straightening up the mess and I'm not done yet."

Winter winds also roar across Yellowstone. They whip snow into blinding ground blizzards and add wind-chill factors to temperatures that often drop very low. Winter readings down to −66° F. have been known, the lowest anywhere in the forty-eight United States. Even on moderate winter days the spray of waterfalls drapes canyon walls with ice, and steam from hot springs freezes against trees and turns them into gigantic ornaments of dazzling crystal. Buffalo pushing through belly-deep snow leave tracks that zigzag across valley bottoms, and beneath aspens and willows snow lies trampled where elk and moose have browsed on bark and shoots.

The Yellowstone River, with its two falls, has cut a canyon 26 miles long.

Snowfall as great as 200 inches can be expected in winter, settling into a blanket about 5 feet deep. More than this falls in parts of the mountains. When summer comes, the snow's melt flows into rivers and lakes, and seeps into enormous natural reservoirs underground. From there it feeds back up to the surface in springs and geysers.

People generally take water as much for granted as the air or the sunshine. Water comes from kitchen faucets. It is to drink, to bathe in, to cook with, and to keep the lawn green through summer's drought. It is to swim in and to water-ski on.

Not so in Yellowstone. There you notice water for its own sake. It is both beautiful and abundant. The Upper Falls of the Yellowstone River drop 109 feet over a cliff, and a half mile farther on the Lower Falls drop 308 feet. These heights are equivalent to plunging from the tenth or the thirtieth story of a city office building. In June, the season when snowmelt reaches its maximum, 64,000 gallons of water pour over with each tick of the clock. This would be like 15,000 fire hoses squirting together full force.

What's more, the water carries enough silt and rocks to constantly erode the river channel, deepening it. The result is a canyon 26 miles long cut into the yellow volcanic rock that gives the park its name. Indians called this gorge "the one with yellow, nearly vertical walls," and Frenchmen who came into the region to trap for furs heard the name and shortened it to *"Pierre Jaune"* or *"Roche Jaune."* In English this means "Yellow Stone" or "Yellow Rock."

Rivers thread the entire park. They flow foaming and hurried in places. They also slip along quietly in parts of their courses, dotted with ducks, geese, and swans. Lakes are important, too. The largest in the park is Yellowstone Lake, which stretches 20 miles long and 14 miles wide. It is larger than any other mountain lake in the United States outside Alaska and Hawaii. Powerboats race across most of its waters, but only canoes, kayaks, and rowboats are allowed on its southern arms. There, you can paddle close to shore watching for moose and beaver. At Heart Lake you can watch a geyser spout while you walk the shore casting for trout, and at Shoshone Lake you can camp where a bubbling hot spring sings an all-night lullaby and warms the water of one particular cove to just the right temperature for a morning swim.

All of Yellowstone's water, and all the water on earth, has recycled itself constantly since the creation of our planet. In that long-ago time when the earth had first formed and begun to cool, cracks opened in its surface and gases were released into the atmosphere. Hydrogen and oxygen atoms from these gases locked together and formed vapor. This caused water droplets and snow to swaddle the infant planet, although none fell to the ground. The earth's surface was too hot. Rain kept getting changed back into vapor before it could touch the land.

The cooling continued, and in time rain began to reach the earth's surface. It fell without stopping for centuries. Rivers, lakes, and oceans formed, but the amount of water did not change. Its form continually changed, but the total amount of water stayed the same. It went from vapor to liquid and, eventually, also to solid in the form of ice. This is the supply of water that we still have today, no more and no less. Some has seeped into the ground. Some lies on the earth's surface. Some rides the air currents and will fall again as rain or snow, sleet or hail.

It's part of an unending cycle, and within the cycle Yellowstone's waters seem almost like a museum collection. The settings are spectacular and the water itself is absolutely pure. Ponds, lakes, and rivers are clear. Their shores and banks are cloaked with willows and grasses, pines and flowers, just as they always have been.

Sadly, the same is not true for the waters of the nation—or the world—as a whole. A river in Ohio carries such a load of oily waste that it regularly catches fire. In Lake Erie, fish have died by the thousands. The Los Angeles River flows captive in a concrete trough. The Columbia lies placid behind a series of dams. Wildlife in the Florida Everglades is threatened because water is diverted for agriculture. Some of these changes have been made on purpose and are helpful to human society. Others are heedless and destructive. Either way, the waters have lost their naturalness. Yellowstone's have not. They are as much a part of the park's great chain of life as they ever have been.

The largest population of native cutthroat trout in the world belongs to Yellowstone, particularly to Yellowstone Lake and the upper river. These are not hatchery raised or artificially fed. They are present because the ecosystem of the lake is in balance. Man has not tampered with streams where females lay their eggs. Shade still cools the shallows and soil is not disturbed. This helps in two ways. The water is not overloaded with silt, which smothers life. At the same time, the undisturbed banks let nutrients leach into the lake. Aquatic insects and tiny shrimplike organisms can thrive and they, in turn, are available as food for the cutthroat.

Native grayling and whitefish swim in other park waters, just as they always have, and with them are rainbow, brown, lake, and brook trout. These were not originally found in the park but were brought in by men decades ago to improve sport fishing. There are also chub, shiners, and sculpins—small fish spurned by man but needed by larger fish and birds as food.

White pelicans nesting on islands in Yellowstone Lake devour hundreds of thousands of fish each year. Without such an abundant source they would have to abandon their nesting ground. Ospreys and bald eagles soar above rivers, then drop to the water and make catches with their talons. Mergansers paddle and dive after fish. Otter and mink rely on them, and even grizzly bears wade into the shallows and catch trout by swatting with their forepaws or by a quick and well-aimed thrust with their jaws. Man fishes in Yellowstone too, but the seasons when he may do so, the size of his catches, and the locations he may use now take second place to the needs of the park's wildlife.

Pelicans must fish for their living, so man now limits his catch to avoid disastrous competition.

Fire and Ice

THE GEOLOGIC STORY OF YELLOWSTONE BEGINS WITH VOLCAN-
ism. For 5 or 10 million years, successive periods of eruption
came one after another. Then there was a long period of quiet,
followed by another fiery round of eruptions. This new epi-
sode was particularly violent. In fact, no upheavals within re-
corded history anywhere in the world begin to approach its
catastrophic destruction. This includes Java's Krakatoa,
which erupted in 1883 with a roar loud enough to be heard
3,000 miles away in Australia, and Mount Pelée in Marti-
nique, which in 1902 spit out glowing avalanches of ash that
killed 29,000 persons.

In Yellowstone, the devastation began as gas welled from
the earth mixed with fragments of glassy ash. Billowing, hissing clouds raced across the land at speeds believed greater
than 100 miles an hour. The weight of the ash made them hug
the ground, extinguishing all life in their path and blanketing
every contour of the landscape. New layers were added before

old ones could cool and in places deposits built more than one thousand feet thick. The internal heat and weight of the ash were so great that the layers welded themselves into a kind of rock called *tuff*.

These vast outpourings set the stage for the next event. A gigantic dome perhaps 60 or 70 miles across swelled like a blister as the gas and *magma,* or molten rock, pushed up from deep within the earth. It roofed a fiery reservoir that kept pouring itself out in eruptions. Eventually, the reservoir emptied. The dome no longer was supported, and it weakened. About 750,000 years ago it collapsed, leaving a hole so big it is almost beyond imagining. Parts of the walls still can be traced and from them it is plain that the *caldera,* as such craters are properly called, measured 50 miles wide and 1 mile deep. It formed in the same way as the caldera that holds Crater Lake, Oregon. But Crater Lake measures only 5 miles across. This is a fraction of the Yellowstone caldera's size.

About 150,000 years after the first caldera formed in Yellowstone, a second, somewhat smaller one formed in the same way. The collapsing of each dome set off new eruptions. Ash flows again burst from cracks in the earth and rushed across the land adding to the devastation.

Next, came a different cycle of eruptions. Lava issued from fractures around the edge of the calderas, but the old pressures were gone. Instead of clouds of ash racing along, these thick flows moved slowly, creeping over the land in great, steep-sided tongues as much as 30 miles long. The rock was molten, but it also was so sticky that it needed to build to a thickness of a thousand feet before it had enough force to move. Geologists think these may have been the thickest and stickiest lava flows in all the world. Some crusted over, then broke and flowed on when new upwellings poured from the earth. Great chunks of lava that had cooled and hardened were carried along on these fresh flows, and when the mixture finally stopped, it formed lumpy cliffs and plateaus.

Some lava was nearly liquid. It flowed at a temperature as high as 1,500° F., yet it often cooled and hardened quickly. This formed obsidian, a smooth and shiny black rock also called *volcanic glass*. Indians prized this kind of stone for making into arrowheads and other weapons, and for tools that needed sharp edges. Obsidian from Yellowstone has been found as far away as Ohio and the Mississippi Valley; and a chunk that weighed 20 pounds was discovered in a burial mound in Illinois. All these pieces of stone can be recognized as being from Yellowstone because of certain trace minerals that exactly match those of Obsidian Cliff in the park. Each flow throughout the world has individual characteristics, which permit identification somewhat as people can be identified by their fingerprints. No two flows and no two sets of fingerprints are ever alike.

How the pieces of obsidian made their way across the plains from Yellowstone nobody knows. They are found in both ancient and recent Indian campsites and burials. Perhaps the shining stone was traded from group to group. Perhaps certain bands made long pilgrimages to obtain it. We probably will never know.

Ice has alternated with fire in shaping Yellowstone. In fact, glaciers had come and gone before the most recent rounds of volcanism began. This is known because gravel laid down by melting ice is found covered with ash. The combination forms a record that geologists can read as plainly as a page in a book. The glaciers of the park were part of ice sheets that have spread across North America at least four times, reaching as far south as Illinois and Ohio. Simultaneously with these glaciations, icecaps also blanketed Europe and Asia. On all three continents they long ago melted almost entirely, but signs of their presence remain.

For example, slabs of rock found in many parts of the world clearly show polishing by some enormous weight. Nobody knew how the polishing got there, then just over a century ago the puzzle was figured out in the Swiss Alps. Men noticed that polishing and scratching, far down the mountainsides from any ice, looked the same as polishing and scratching on rock newly melted free at the edges of existing glaciers. They realized that the polishing must have come from the slow movement of past ice riding over the rock, and the scratches from the rasping of pebbles locked in its bottom.

Another major sign that ice once covered vast areas is found in erratics, scattered boulders that were transported by ice, then dropped as it melted. Rocks from the size of a crate to as big as a garage can be seen riding the surface of today's gla-

Huge boulders carried by an ancient glacier now dot the Lamar Valley.

ciers and down in their crevasses. The same sort of thing happened in the past. Erratics and ice-polished rocks dot Central Park in New York City. They lie on the top of Cadillac Mountain in Maine and across the wheat fields of eastern Washington. There are other signatures of ice, too. Bunker Hill in Boston was shaped by ice. So were the lakes of Minnesota.

There is evidence that temperatures once were arctic in several places where the climate now is mild. Reindeer antlers have turned up in deposits along the coast of the Mediterranean Sea, and arctic fox bones have been found throughout Europe and as far south as Washington and Wisconsin on the North American continent. These animals can live only in extremely cold climates, so discovering their bones tells a great deal about past conditions. Wherever they once lived it must have been cold at the time.

The ocean gives similar indications of great cold in past ages. A remarkable method of reading the chemistry of shells makes this certain. The calcium carbonate that many shells are made of is a chemical compound of calcium, carbon, and oxygen, with its exact characteristics depending on the temperature of the water at the time the shell formed. Study of many shells shows periods when the ocean must have been colder than it is today.

The Yellowstone glaciers shielded all but the highest peaks in the park region at least twice, and perhaps three times. They started in the high mountains, particularly in the Absaroka Range along the eastern boundary of the park. Snow fell steadily, more than could melt during the brief summers that brought feeble warmth to the land. It piled deep and compacted into ice. Pressures within began to mount, and in time they became great enough to cause movement. The ice inched forward. It sculptured cliffs and ridges as it moved, and

Ice once blanketed all but the highest peaks of the Absaroka Range.

it rounded the tops of mountains that stood in its path. It polished rocks and left erratic boulders easily seen today in the Lamar Valley and near Yellowstone Canyon.

Nearly 4,000 square miles of the land in and around Yellowstone lay beneath ice during the maximum of the last ice age, perhaps twenty or thirty thousand years ago. In places the ice cap was more than half a mile thick. It was such an immense amount that, even after it quit moving and began to melt, it continued to affect the land. Great chunks of dying glaciers blocked runoff from the ice itself and from snowstorms and rainstorms. Ponds formed, held by the ice dams. Streams flowing into them brought sediment, which settled to the bottom. Gradually the ponds turned into marshes, and eventually into meadows. Today, you can find geese and elk grazing in these meadows—but the grass they feed on is there because of the glaciers.

In places, ice chunks were separated from the main glacier and became buried by gravel and silt. Many were so well insulated that they lasted for centuries before melting, and at least one seems not to have melted yet. It was discovered in 1931 by a crew of men building a road near Tower Junction in the northern park. As they scraped, near the base of a cliff, they uncovered ice! It lay beneath 2 feet of rock rubble. The color was blue gray and the texture was hard and glassy, characteristics typical of glacier ice. Apparently, this piece is left from the ice age that ended about twelve thousand years ago in the Yellowstone region.

The buried chunk is huge. Its full size was not determined, but it ran for at least 600 feet along the roadway and perhaps farther. The exact length wasn't measured. Neither was any attempt made to see how far out to the side of the cliff the ice reached, or how deep into the ground. At the time, the men's only interest was in building the road. They simply covered the ice with gravel and continued the asphalting. Nobody has gone back since to investigate, but the ice must still be there. The road keeps sinking at that particular point and needing repair! The underlying ice evidently is slowly melting, causing the surface of the land to drop.

The climate in Yellowstone during the last thousands of years couldn't possibly have produced such ice. This mammoth chunk must date from the ice age—and incredibly long ago as that seems in one sense, it is very recent if you think of it in another way. In our individual human lives, nothing can possibly happen more than eighty or one hundred years ago, and usually not quite that much. That is as long as we live. But in terms of written history, the past covers thousands of years, instead of one hundred; and the prehistory that archaeologists probe stretches still farther into the past. Yet, even this isn't long if you compare the full time of man's existence against the age of the earth itself. Our species is believed to be about 2.5 million years old—and this is the merest tick of the clock compared to the 5 billion years since the earth formed. Furthermore, even geologic time is as nothing compared to cosmic time, the scale that astronomers work with.

The immensity of such measurements is too far beyond human experience to let us have much feeling of what the numbers represent. It helps if you let the height of the Empire State Building in New York City represent the age of the earth. Place a nickel on top of it, and the thickness of the coin will represent the age of mankind. That is what 5 billion is like in comparison to 2.5 million.

On this scale, Yellowstone's buried ice becomes recent instead of ancient. So do even the earliest eruptions in the park. They date from 50 million years ago, but the earth is 100 times that old.

Geysers

YELLOWSTONE IS STILL HOT. THE VOLCANIC FIRES OF THE past have not gone out. Magma at temperatures as high as 1700° F. probably lies less than 2 miles below the surface, and this heat causes something like 10,000 hot springs, geysers, mud pots, and steam vents. There are more hot-water features here than in all the rest of the world combined. All are active year-round, no matter what the season or the weather. Their water comes mostly from snowmelt. It seeps through cracks and is stored in loose deposits of glacial rubble. A little of the water is from a different source. It is a kind termed *juvenile water,* which means that it forms for the first time from hydrogen and oxygen atoms present in the magma. Such new water is rare anywhere in the world, and in Yellowstone it amounts to only 3 or 4 percent of the water supply for hot springs and geysers.

Thermal features don't look much alike from one type to another. Even so the basic cause for them all is the release of heat

Castle Geyser is one of several geysers in the Old Faithful basin.
Bob and Ira Spring

Mud pots often form around steam vents where water has collected.

from within the earth. They are *geothermal*. *Geo* means "earth," and *thermal* means "heat." Four types are found in Yellowstone. The simplest are vents, from which steam and other gases escape directly out of the earth. Sometimes the steam comes as frail wisps, sometimes as billowing and hissing plumes.

Mud pots, a second type of geothermal feature, are an elaboration of steam vents. Their underground structure is about the same except that it flares at the top to form a bowl-like depression where rain and snow collect. Escaping gases rise through the water, bringing sulfur, which combines with the water to make sulfuric acid. The acid breaks down the rock of the basin into clay, and the result is soupy mud with gas bubbling through it. Mud pots may be 3 or 4 feet in diameter, or may measure as much as 50 feet across. Bubbles swell like balloons at their surface, then burst into threads and blobs of

Opal Terrace has been built from minerals deposited by the water of Mammoth Hot Springs.

mud. The sound is like a gigantic pot of simmering oatmeal with added deep booms and gurgles, intense hissing, and a percussion of clicks and splats.

Hot springs form as heated water rises to the surface and collects in pools. Some are so hot they are boiling. Many are colorful, as their names suggest—Emerald Hot Spring, Pearl, Opal, Sapphire, even Rainbow. Greens and blues seem the most frequent, but brown, gray, red, and yellow springs also are present. Sometimes the color comes from minerals coating the walls of the spring, or suspended in the water. Most often, it is simply from the way the pool acts as a prism and refracts light within the water. One spring is named Grand Prismatic because of its remarkable range of colors. This is a large pool, 370 feet across. The center is deep blue, lightening and shifting to turquoise and green away from the center, then continuing through the spectrum with rings of yellow, orange, and red toward the edge. On chilly days a cloud of steam hangs above Grand Prismatic and all the colors reflect on its underside, giving a double view of their brilliance.

Geysers are basically hot springs except that they have more intricate plumbing systems. Pressures mount so high that water shoots out explosively. Old Faithful, the most popular geyser of all, long ago became the symbol of the park. It shoots out 10,000 gallons of water in from 2 to 5 minutes, a great column of water that lifts more than 100 feet into the air. Nobody knows how deeply Old Faithful is rooted. It has been probed for nearly 600 feet but the inner "pipes" of a geyser are far from straight or simple. They are a network of twisting cracks and cavities that feed into each other at every possible angle. Because of this there is no way to know how far the probe dropped vertically. Much of the 600 feet may have been a horizontal measurement.

Every hour or so, Old Faithful shoots out water, although the periods between eruptions have been as short as 33 minutes and as long as 148 minutes. The usual interval is a fairly dependable 55 to 65 minutes. The temperature of the water (204° F.) and the amount (10,000 to 12,000 gallons per eruption) also tend to hold steady.

Constant temperature and volume are true for most geysers. So is the way they build and release pressure. Each holds to its own particular pattern, although most differ greatly from one another and, unlike Old Faithful, don't necessarily have regularly timed eruptions. Some geysers spout nearly all the time. Others seem to be on cycles, with eruptions days, months, or even years apart.

Consider Steamboat Geyser as an example. It erupted five times before 1911, then not at all for fifty years. In 1961 there was an outburst, and three years after that activity built to a frenzy with 29 major eruptions. Each lasted for hours. Water shot 380 feet, far higher than any other geyser in the park, and the roar was so deafening that men watching an eruption couldn't hear each other even when they shouted. But after a few years, activity dwindled to mere splashing 20 or 30 feet high. Maybe the interior plumbing of the geyser gutted itself and destroyed the system at least temporarily. Steamboat Geyser may never again produce a dramatic show, or it may erupt tomorrow and outdo its previous record. Nobody knows what to expect, but Yellowstone visitors who are fans of Steamboat keep vigil whenever they can, on the chance that they will be on hand when the next eruption stirs.

Regardless of size or frequency, the physics of all eruptions are the same. One geyser system may draw on enormous supplies of water and send up thousands of gallons at a time. Another may have only a small vent and a modest amount of water. It will erupt with a burst of spray instead of a fountain of water. No matter. The inner workings differ only in the fine details.

Nobody has ever gone down into a geyser or excavated one to discover how it works. However, from observations of what happens at the surface, scientists have pieced together what must be taking place below ground. Enormous heat always is involved. It comes from the magma, which heats overlying rocks. These in turn heat water that is in contact with them. In Norris Geyser Basin, researchers have drilled deep holes and tested water temperatures. Their thermometers read as high as 465° F. and actual temperatures may go to 706° F., the highest point at which water can stay liquid. Above that, it becomes gas.

Such temperatures are possible because of pressure. The principle is about the same as that of a pressure kettle used for

cooking. Because the kettle is sealed, pressure builds and temperatures rise higher than is possible without the seal. Instead of boiling at 212° F., as is standard at sea level in an unsealed pot, water will boil at a higher temperature. How high depends on how much pressure there is.

Deep in the earth, pressures are so great that even superheated water cannot boil. However, its heat makes it rise and, as it does, the pressure on it drops. Eventually it reaches a point where it can boil. When this happens bubbles begin to form. There are so many of them and they keep expanding so fast that they can't all escape through the geyser's narrow tubes and cracks. Some of the water is forced up and spurts out. This reduces pressure on the rest of the water and it suddenly explodes into steam. The space that steam needs is hundreds of times greater than water needs as liquid. This forces more water out the top—and the eruption is on.

How long it lasts depends on how much water there is. When the next eruption will be depends on how quickly the geyser's reservoir is replenished and how soon the heat and pressure rebuild.

Thermal features such as Grotto Geyser, above, and White Dome Geyser, right, draw their water from underground reservoirs held by glacial gravels and fed by rain runoff and snowmelt.

Heat and Life

FLOWERS BLOOM MONTHS EARLIER IN THE GEYSER BASINS than in the rest of the park. The heat in the ground melts snow as fast as it falls, and this keeps plants from being blanketed by snow. It also provides them with moisture. One kind of small plant, called spurge, blossoms year-round. By growing on the hot ground and hugging it like a mat, this plant lives in a tropical environment even when the temperature has dropped to below zero a few feet away, beyond the geyser basin. Monkey flower and mustard also profit from hot ground. They are plants that ordinarily die back in winter, but where they grow close to geysers they carry rosettes of leaves over the winter, and when April comes they are ready for a burst of growth. They simply lengthen their shoots and bloom, long before any other plants in the park have started to flower.

One species of pearly everlasting grows in thermal basins and nowhere else. It *must* have heat. In fact, it often grows right in the mouth of a gently steaming vent. A few mosses and

Wild geranium

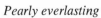
Pearly everlasting

Fringed gentian

Cone flower

Increasing thermal activity caused Sour Lake to expand and kill trees around it.

lichens live at the edges of hot springs, warmed by air blowing off the water. If the wind reverses and brings frigid air from the surrounding areas, they freeze. Only species able to endure ice crystals in their cells can live in these locations.

One of the first signs that the temperature of a thermal basin is changing will be changes in the vegetation. If hot springs start getting hotter, or steam vents or geysers that have been quiet start stirring back to life, lodgepole pines seem to foretell the increasing heat. They set an extra heavy crop of cones before the human eye can notice any sign of change in the ground. The individual trees are doomed by the increased heat, but their superabundant seeds assure continuation of the species. Wherever hot ground is advancing into the forest, successive rings of dry grass, and dead and dying trees mark its spread. Or, where a meadow that has been hot is beginning to cool, seedlings of lodgepole again sprout and start turning the

When the ground of a thermal basin cools, lodgepole pine can grow again.

bare soil back into shady forest. In time, birds will nest and deer and elk will come to bed down for the night.

Worldwide, the earth's surface averages 54° F., but geologists and astronomers speak of much hotter temperatures for our planet in the past. Could there have been life then? What temperature was acceptable? Answers may come from the study of hot springs in Yellowstone. A few years ago a biologist working in the park suspended glass slides into a 204-degree spring, a temperature 6 degrees hotter than boiling at Yellowstone's elevation. He couldn't see any life in the bubbling water, but within a week the slides were coated with jellylike threads of bacteria. These are a single-celled type of primitive plant. Similar bacteria were known in springs below boiling temperatures. So were algae, another primitive form of plant. But this was the first time that living organisms had been discovered in water hotter than boiling.

The bacteria made the researcher wonder why they were there. Was the high temperature best for them to grow in? Or was it that such scalding water meant they didn't have to compete with other plants or risk being eaten by aquatic insects or fish? To find the answer, he placed samples of bacteria into vials and then moved them from springs of one temperature to another. In every case, growth was best at the temperature where the bacteria had been living originally. In just three hours the cells would swell and divide in two; in another three hours each of them would divide, and so on—a rapid growth rate in spite of the extreme heat.

If more can be learned, it may be possible to discover how high the temperature can go before life stops and also what causes heat to limit life. Nobody knows about this yet, but the answers may well come from Yellowstone. Life thrives there at higher temperatures than anywhere else, including the other hot spring areas of the world.

Mats of bacteria and algae give brilliant color to thermal pools and runoff channels. The bacteria string together as threads of pale pink covered with a gelatinlike sheath. The algae come in greens and blues, yellows and oranges, depending on the water temperatures and on how much light there is. When winter shortens the days and lessens the sunshine, the green of the algae in Yellowstone's hot springs increases. The plants need more chlorophyll—the green substance in plants' cells—to make up for the loss of light. (Chlorophyll is the pigment that plants use to absorb light energy used in photosynthesis, which converts carbon dioxide and water into sugar and other plant materials.)

Water temperatures do not vary with the season. The springs are born of a deep-earth system far too vast to be influenced by weather changes sweeping across the surface of the earth.

Only two surface conditions can drastically affect a hot spring. One is getting trampled by buffalo or elk. The other is violent pounding by hail. Yet even when a storm completely strips the algae and bacteria mats from a spring, growth begins anew within about a week and in five months time all is back to normal.

Members of the animal kingdom are present in scalding water, as well as the bacteria and algae. However, animal life can live only up to temperatures of about 140° F., nowhere near the full extreme endured by plants. The most noticeable of the animals are flies belonging to the *Ephydridae* family. These are brine flies, a kind found in highly salty and oily pools as well as in hot springs throughout the world. They feed on algae at the surface of the water and underneath it. A bubble of air held by bristly hairs covering their bodies protects them from the heat while they walk around under the water. On the coldest winter days and in the midst of bitter snowstorms, the flies can continue feeding, mating, and laying eggs. Their world is limited to the water and an inch or two above it, but so long as they stay within these boundaries the conditions they experience hold warm and steady.

Other kinds of flies live parasitically on the brine flies and their larvae. So do red mites. The flies and mites in turn furnish food for other forms of life. Spiders and carabid beetles patrol the edges of hot-spring pools and channels, ready to dash out momentarily and capture a meal. Dragonflies hover above the springs to prey on the spiders, mites, and flies (but not the beetles, which are too hard). Birds feed on the dragonflies, the spiders, the mites and the flies—and on other insects that mistakenly come too close to the water and meet their death because of the heat. Snipes warm themselves by a vent of wispy steam, then stride after insects. Seedeaters such as spar-

Elk spend the winter in Firehole Basin which is kept fairly free of snow by underground heat.

rows and rosy finches hop along the green edges of hot-water rivulets harvesting food from plants.

Ice can't form where hot springs flow into Yellowstone Lake, Yellowstone River, and other park waters. This lets thousands of waterfowl congregate for the winter. Canada geese graze steamy banks kept free of snow by the heat. Trumpeter swans arch their long necks under the water to feed on bottom plants. Pelicans dive after fish. Golden-eye ducks swim in great flocks and when they take flight their wings squeak loudly. Mink feed on the ducks through the winter. Beaver and muskrat find enough plant food to stay active year-round.

In March, bears come out of hibernation and head for geyser basins to break their long fasts. Most of the park still lies deep in snow, but in the basins, shrews and mice are sure to be found; there are logs to break open for grubs, and fleshy

Coyotes patrol the park for carrion and for rodents and small birds.

roots to dig from the meadows. Elk stay throughout the winter in Firehole Basin, and for bears that means the promise of an early spring meal of warm flesh. In any of the thermal areas the chances of finding carrion are good. Coyotes and bobcats, as well as bears, patrol these areas seeking the carcass of a winter-killed elk or buffalo to feed on as supplement for a diet of unwary rodents or birds.

Fish seem unaffected by the scalding water pouring into Yellowstone's rivers. Evidently it quickly chills as it merges with the icy flow of a river, for trout have been found within a few feet of hot-spring runoffs at temperatures as high as 200° F. The major effect on fish seems to be beneficial. The heat fosters an increased food supply by providing a longer growing season for aquatic organisms. Elsewhere hot water often harms fish. Industries and power-generating plants in many parts of the world pour heated water into rivers and lakes, and because the heat is unnatural it poses serious problems.

Warmer temperatures have been found responsible for bacterial disease among some species of fish. Salmon stimulated by the warmth have spawned out of season. Heat has acted as a barrier, cutting off upriver migration routes. Higher temperatures have affected the salmon's metabolism. For example, each 10-degree rise causes fish studied in the Columbia River to double the oxygen they use, which is a serious problem since warm water holds less oxygen than cold water does. This means that the fish need more oxygen than normal, but they get less. In Yellowstone, gushing hot water is a natural part of the environment and it sets off no distortion. But, where heat flowing into rivers is not natural, life can't readily adjust to its effects.

The thermal basins of the park give refuge to wildlife and they also spell death at times. Rock crusts around geysers and hot pools often form thin brittle rims that may reach for 10 or 20 feet. Buffalo and elk are too heavy for these crusts to hold. They break through and drop to their deaths in the boiling water. Tragically, so do humans. Occasionally someone disregards warning signs and strays off the boardwalks that lead through the thermal basins. Some have fallen into pools and been killed, others have been badly burned.

Poisonous gases are another hazard. People, once in a while, get headaches and wildlife, especially birds, sometimes die. A total of 236 dead birds were counted one year on the terraces of Mammoth Hot Springs alone. Carbon dioxide bubbles up in springs there and rises through steam vents. It is heavier than air and collects in pockets. Birds coming to roost or to drink are overcome and die. This happens so commonly that coyotes make a daily check of certain crevices. They know better than

In winter, buffalo come to hot springs to warm themselves and to graze.

to linger long, but they also know that a quick check is likely to bring a ready-made meal of a warbler, sparrow or junco.

Left to itself, nature easily fits its pieces together, even oddities like extreme heat and poisonous gases. To men, Yellowstone's thermal features seem extraordinary because we know how rare they are. But for the birds and animals that live in the park they are simply part of the home environment. The heat can be avoided or utilized depending on circumstances. If death comes to an individual because of scalding water, or gas, others will find life. Nature loses nothing. The flesh of the fallen quickly goes to sustain the living.

The Forests

THE LAND SURFACE OF YELLOWSTONE IS CLOTHED WITH FOR-
ests, and evidently this has been true for an exceedingly long
time. A single ridge, called Specimen Ridge, has 27 forests of
stones standing one on top of another like a gigantic layer
cake. Hike there and you find yourself walking through an
ordinary Douglas-fir forest, clothing today's surface. Buried
underneath your feet are the other, ancient ones.

Other ridges in the northern park are similarly layered by
petrified trees, although Specimen Ridge shows what happened
especially well. Volcanism dictated the fate of the forests.
About 50 million years ago rifts in the earth poured out lava
all across the Rocky Mountain region, including Yellowstone.
Most of the park area was a series of low, forested valleys
bounded by hills and dotted with volcanic cones at that time,
and whenever one of the cones exploded it sent hot ash billowing into the air. Steam hissed with a deafening roar, making
the whole area like a monstrous sauna bath. Glowing blobs of

Forests cover the peaks and valleys of Yellowstone today, as in the past.

molten rock rained to earth in a deadly storm that broke the branches from trees and suffocated roots as the pores of the soil became clogged. Rivers were choked. They no longer could drain the land. Instead, rain runoff mixed with loose ash and lava, and hot soupy mud spread across the land. The forest stood silent. Only its tree trunks rose above the volcanic blanket, and they were bare.

Today, scientists are studying the remains of the ancient forest and they have pieced together what happened. The trees still are standing upright, therefore it seems likely that the devastation came slowly. Mud flows buried and choked plants without uprooting them, and ash filled the air. It coated leaves and caused them to wither and fall. Sometimes rain mixed with the ash and formed acids, which dropped as a killing mist. Leaves that have turned to stone are found still curled, just as they fell from the trees. Wildlife had time to flee. No bird or

Petrified tree trunks stand on Specimen Ridge, part of 27 successive forests, one on top of another.

animal bones are found except for field mice.

The climate at the time of the eruptions must have been warm and moist, about like Florida or Louisiana today, to judge by the vegetation of the ancient forests. There were sycamore, walnut, magnolia, oak, and dogwood trees; also climbing ferns, hickories, and bayberries—species altogether different from Yellowstone's evergreen forest today. Cells from the buried trees still can be identified under a microscope, even now millions of years after the smothering ashfalls and mud flows. The wood is petrified. Hot water dissolved minerals from the volcanic debris that covered the forest. As it seeped into the dead trunks, twigs and leaves, the minerals filled the cells and the wood slowly turned to stone. Fine details such as cell structure and annual growth rings were preserved, and these are what experts can recognize today. They tell what the ancient forest was like.

Nobody can say how long after an eruption it took for a new forest to replace a buried one. The first pioneering plants may have sprouted quickly. This has happened after eruptions elsewhere. At Paricutín in Mexico, a few years ago, a volcano showered the land with ash, yet just a month later observers found green shoots. A cementlike crust capped the ash but there were breaks in its surface, and plants flourished in them. The same was true at Katmai, Alaska. Eruptions in 1912 filled a valley with ash 700 feet deep, turning it as sterile as the moon. Yet only a few weeks later, the tracks of a bear crossing the new surface were so tinted with green that they looked as if the bear had been stepping in paint. The color came from lupine plants. Seeds had caught in each footprint and sprouted.

Lupine is especially well suited for this kind of pioneering. Its seeds are heavy enough to lodge wherever there is a crack instead of blowing on. Also, they are rich with nutrients needed by the sprouting plants until their roots have time to develop. Furthermore, lupines belong to a group of plants known as *legumes*. These can draw nitrogen from the air instead of depending on it to be already in the soil. Since all plants need nitrogen, this ability is particularly valuable for species invading barren soil, whether the gravel of a river bar or the ashen debris of a volcanic eruption.

Some of Yellowstone's new forests may have reclothed the land as quickly as forty or fifty years following destruction of an old one. Others probably took two or three hundred years, depending on particulars of climate and soil. Either way, slow or fast, plants turned the land green again after each eruption. Then new fissures would open and volcanic flows would engulf the forest again. Over and over the pattern repeated itself.

Today, three-quarters of the park is covered with lodgepole pine, a species that often grows like tall poles almost without branches except at the top. Such trees may be little more than 3 inches in diameter although one hundred or two hundred years old and fully mature. The name comes from this spindly characteristic. Indians used the trunks as frameworks for their tepees, fastening on animal hides to complete the dwellings. They also leaned dozens of the poles together to form lodges that didn't need to be covered with skins.

Lodgepole pines spring up in the black aftermath of fire. They pioneer areas devastated by flame as readily as they invade cooling thermal basins, or as they once conquered the raw rubble left by Yellowstone's volcanic outbursts and by its dying glaciers. They bear cones that open only about a third of the way when they first mature. This lets a portion of the seeds scatter, but the rest stay inside the cones, sealed shut by pitch. Fire releases them. When the temperature gets around 140° F. the pitch melts and the seeds fall out.

Lodgepole pines grow tall and spindly with few branches except toward the top.

Fire used to be a natural part of the forest cycle, but about fifty or sixty years ago man began developing control methods, and fire all but disappeared in the park. In the early days, Indians had deliberately set fires. Mature forests had little to offer them. Tribesmen fared better after fires had swept an area because with competitors gone a variety of new plants could grow up and animals would come to graze and browse on them. This meant fresh greens to eat as vegetables, berries to dry for winter, and meat to roast and to preserve by drying.

In addition to fires caused by man, lightning often set the forest ablaze. For at least ten thousand years, fire repeatedly swept across Yellowstone, to judge from charcoal found in ancient peat deposits and lake bed sediments and beneath deposits of glacial gravel. Probably no particular part of the forest burned more than once every ten or twenty years, and maybe less often than that. Seeds locked within cones could wait. Lodgepole cones fifty years old have released seeds still capable of sprouting. They are so lightweight that 100,000 of them weigh only a pound. This is characteristic of the seeds of pioneering plants. They must be light enough to ride the wind. After a fire, with no mice left to eat seeds as they fall, as many as 300,000 tiny pines will spring up to an acre. In twenty years, 60,000 of them will remain, now 8 or 10 feet tall. By the end of a century, the count will be down to only 200, but new trees will be coming on.

There is a mystery about the lodgepoles growing in Yellowstone National Park. For some reason, their cones don't seem as dependent on heat for opening as is true for most lodgepoles. Their seeds often shake out as soon as they mature. Biologists think this may have come about because the frequency of fire has dropped. More study is needed before they can be sure, and this is difficult because the trees surrounding the park are cut by loggers, and, therefore, make a poor comparison with the untouched forest inside park boundaries. Men, of course, no longer burn the area (assuming Indians did so here as they are known to have done elsewhere). Fires caused by lightning also may be fewer now than they once were. The possible reason for this is that spruce and fir trees have ceased to grow in Yellowstone in as great numbers as it is believed they once did. Lodgepole has been so successful that the other species cannot compete and grow now only in scattered groves. Without their tall spires acting as lightning rods to draw the fury of thunderclouds to earth, there have been fewer fires. This has resulted, scientists believe, in lodgepole cones no longer needing to be at least partially sealed by pitch. On the contrary, circumstance has favored cones that open without the help of fire.

In time more will be learned. The single century that the land has been a park and closely studied is not long enough to observe all the cycles of nature, let alone, understand them. In the case of fire and its role, cautious experiments in Yellowstone and elsewhere are giving new knowledge. Fires have been started on purpose with crews standing by to keep them from flaring beyond control. The practice sounds reckless but the reason behind the burning is sound. There is growing awareness that forests change continually, left to themselves, and through the ages fire has been a prime agent of this change.

In place of wildfire, men now substitute carefully controlled burning that is timed for certain conditions of weather and of dryness within the forest. In this way they allow natural change to continue. Tender new shoots soon lift from soil freshly cleansed of its blanketing pine needles. Rabbits feed on the shoots and their flesh in turn becomes food for coyotes and

Great horned owls hunt in forest openings for rabbits and mice.

owls. Shrubs offer browse for deer and moose. In ten or fifteen years the new pines start producing cones, and birds such as siskins and crossbills come to pry out their seeds and feed on them. Mice again harvest all seeds they can find on the forest floor, and foxes and weasels pounce on the mice. Through change the forest cycle rebuilds itself.

Eliminating fire comes from thinking in human terms—admiring the forest and fearing fire—rather than from thinking in biological or ecological terms. Commercial forest lands where trees are cut for lumber and pulp are managed as farms with every possible mechanical and chemical control used to improve growing conditions, and with planting, thinning, and harvesting just as for any farm crop. However, this kind of management is not appropriate for wilderness lands that are intended as places where nature is to reign. The new system also calls for letting fires that start naturally burn themselves out whenever possible. Man will interfere only as is necessary to protect buildings, or if a long accumulation of fuel on the forest floor threatens to cause a fire to burn explosively.

Fire affects trees in ways that were not recognized until recently. For example, groves of aspen trees are admired for their white trunks and round leaves that dance in the slightest breeze, yet Yellowstone's aspens seem to be dying out. Instead of starting from seed these trees reproduce *vegetatively*. They send up shoots from the root crown whenever an existing tree is cut by a beaver or severely scorched by fire—and this means that by fighting fire, men unintentionally have been affecting aspens. Biologists decided to test the effect of fire on the trees by burning an area in the northern park. They watched the flames race through an aspen grove, licking at the trunks. A year later they went back to check on what had happened.

They found new shoots ten times as plentiful in the burned area as in the surrounding unburned area. And since the fire had killed sagebrush, sapling firs, and pines, competition was gone. The new aspens stood a good chance of growing into full size-trees—or they would if it weren't for animals finding them tasty. Rodents nipped off one-quarter of the shoots by the time they were barely over a year old, and elk browsed another third of them during the winter.

Elk eat more grass than anything else, but in winters when snow comes early and deep they turn to trees, feeding on needles, twigs, bark, and leaf buds. Throughout the park, aspen shoots don't have a chance to get more than a foot or two high before elk bite them off, and studies show that unless a shoot can grow about 5 inches each year for several years it isn't likely to ever produce a tree. Therefore, the elk have become a threat to the future of the groves. They even affect mature trees, reaching as high as they can to feed on the bark.

Probably none of this was a problem for aspen in primeval times, but in the last century man has upset natural balances. He stopped wildfire, which is one of nature's systems for winding the clock and starting plant communities anew. Without meaning to, he also caused the size of the elk herds in the park to double and triple, and this destroyed the relationship between the amount of browse and the animals needing it. These unnatural changes coming at once nearly destroyed the aspen groves.

Aspen groves have suffered from reduced burning and from overbrowsing by elk.   *Bob and Ira Spring*

Animals

ELK ARE THE MOST COMMON OF THE LARGE ANIMALS IN YEL-
lowstone. They total more in number and in mass of flesh than
all the other grazing animals of the park combined (deer,
moose, antelope, bighorn sheep, and buffalo). Elk dominate.
Their feeding habits drastically affect vegetation, and this in
turn determines the food supply for other animal species.

Sometimes the others have to move on. A few years ago elk
began browsing aspen shoots near a beaver pond. For years
the beaver had been cutting trees to build their dams and
lodges, then feeding on the new shoots that grew from the old
stumps. The supply of building materials and food had stayed
in balance. Then the elk came, too many elk. They cropped
the shoots to mere stubs. None grew into trees anymore, and
the area became unsuitable for beaver. They left. The dams
holding their ponds no longer were maintained. They began to
leak. The water flowed out and sedges that muskrat fed on
couldn't grow. The muskrat moved out too. Ducks stopped

Beaver ponds are home for muskrats and ducks, as well as for the beavers that dam them.

nesting, and weasels that had counted on eggs and fluffy nestlings to nourish their own young had to seek new territories. The foraging of the elk had set off a chain reaction.

The key to the tremendous success of the elk herds in Yellowstone is their wide-ranging appetite. They wade about in marshes feeding on sedges and rushes; they graze in meadows and browse their way through the forest eating bark, needles, and leaves from trees. They adapt to fairly deep snow in valley bottoms, and to windswept open ridges. They can thrive in any part of the park, just as they once ranged the continent from coast-to-coast and from Canada practically to Mexico. They are versatile and this has made them successful.

Perhaps 15,000 elk now spend the summer in Yellowstone, a brief season of abundant food and mild temperatures. Then comes winter. When its icy hold is clamped onto the land the herds move to lower country—and until recently this created a problem. Men also need the land, and because there are ranches, mines, logging operations, and villages everywhere outside the park, the winter world of the elk vanished.

Only Yellowstone offered food through the winter, and herds began staying in the park all year. This was hard on the plants, and the range began to show abuse. Yellowstone is a natural summer home for elk, but it can't support them all in winter. Many animals couldn't find food enough, but even so there wasn't any place else to go. Elk that did try to move onto their old wintering grounds were shot at by hunters lining the north boundary of the park. (No hunting is permitted in the park.)

For a time Yellowstone elk lost their winter range and were forced to stay inside the park year-round.

This situation had developed slowly over a long period of time. When Yellowstone was established as a national park in 1872 it was the largest remaining stronghold of America's elk herds. The public wanted them to be "helped" in every way possible. Wolves and mountain lions in the park were killed to protect elk against attack, and hay was raised as winter feed. The herds increased, but when winter came elk often died by the hundreds or fell victim to disease or to predators. Rangers tried to prevent the deaths by reducing the size of the herds. They trapped elk and shipped them to states wanting to re-establish herds. They also shot elk and gave the meat to Indian tribes and schools for their hot lunch programs.

Even so, every few years winter brought widespread death —and actually this was normal. Die-offs of this type relieve the pressure on the land. Food supplies can build back. Herds then regain strength and balance returns. Such cycles must have been the pattern through all the long centuries before the establishment of the park. Men realize this now, and the accepted way to help elk is to leave them alone. Land along the north boundary has been added to the park to restore winter feeding grounds, and additional refuges have been established outside the park. Hunting seasons are set late enough to let the herds make their migration in peace.

Inside the park, elk are left alone. If winter comes early and lasts long, one-quarter of the herd may perish. To humans this may seem sad, or wasteful, but it actually furthers nature's overall scheme. Most of the deaths are calves too weak to fight the cold and snow. Only the hardy survive, and from the herd's standpoint this is good. It assures that the vigorous genes of the strongest animals will be the ones passed on. Surprisingly, mature bulls die the next most often, after the calves, and this too works well for the future. During the fall mating season,

In fall, bull elk are busy fighting and mating, and may fail to put on enough fat for the winter.

the bulls are so busy fighting and breeding that they don't feed well. They fail to build a reserve of flesh and fat to carry them through winter. Cows and younger bulls put on weight, but actively breeding bulls lose weight. They are the monarchs of autumn, but they enter winter in poor condition and are eliminated. Younger, stronger bulls seek out the cows and take over the perpetuation of the herd when the next breeding season comes.

The elk that die are not wasted. Their flesh assures the well-being of meat-eating species. Grizzly bears coming out of hibernation and urgently in need of a meal occasionally run down stragglers and kill them with a crushing, shaking bite at the neck. Mountain lions and wolves also cull the weak from the herds, and species such as coyotes, lynx, wolverines, and even mice feed on elk that have starved or frozen to death. Birds join the feast, too. In fact, the fluttering of ravens and magpies is a sign that biologists look for as a mark of a fallen elk. In about 48 hours every trace of a carcass will disappear except for bloodstained, trampled snow and a few bones and bits of hide that have been dragged a short way and dropped. The individual elk has lost its life, but the herd continues. Furthermore, the flesh of the one serves the need of the wild life community as a whole. It is nature's way, and no species except man finds it cruel.

Elk need to get away from deep snow. They can't run well when it piles more than 2 or 3 feet deep, and pawing trenches to feed on hidden grasses and sedges becomes increasingly slow and hard. To avoid the problem now, most again move to lower country outside the park for the winter. However, one herd of about 1,000 has no need to migrate. It lives near the Firehole River. Grazing territory for these elk includes geyser basins where geothermal heat keeps the ground fairly free of snow. February grazing isn't as luxuriant as July's, but it is enough.

A separate, much smaller band solves the problem of winter food in another way. As the first blizzards howl into Yellowstone in October, they start moving to higher country, not lower. They seek the mountain slopes of the park's northwest corner where temperatures are bitterly cold but winds sweep aside enough of the snow to permit grazing on dry grass left from summer. There these elk spend the winter.

Mule deer and antelope meet winter's test by avoiding snow as much as possible. They are physiologically able to endure periods of subzero temperatures, but they are poorly equipped to deal with heavy snow. Their legs are short compared to elk's and they haven't the strength to fight deep drifts. They flounder and fall prey to bobcats, mountain lions, and wolves. Consequently the low-elevation sagebrush flats along the north boundary of the park are their preferred wintering place. Dried

Bighorn sheep spend the winter on high, windswept slopes where snow seldom lies deep.

grass is available part of the time and brush is constantly within reach as browse.

Bighorn sheep stay among the cliffs, able to scramble about wherever forage is available. Buffalo swing their massive heads from side to side and plow clearings through snow 3 or 4 feet deep, reaching down for grass. Each of these wildlife species depends on plant food to fuel their bodies through the winter, which lasts five or six months in Yellowstone. In summer, they spread out widely, but winter's snow holds them concentrated onto only 10 or 20 percent of the park's land. Even so, balance is maintained. The animals' preferences for food and their ability to find it in winter vary enough to control competition. Each species fills its own niche.

Moose cope easily. Their long legs help them push through deep snow and their favorite diet consists of leaves, twigs, and bark, so winter can't cover their food. Moose need only to rear onto their hind legs and pull down fresh supplies of aspen,

With their long legs, moose can rear up and pull browse from trees.

willow, or fir to feed on. In winter, the branches are brittle with cold and they usually crack and stay down. This puts them within reach of hares, which also are browsers and might be hard pressed to find enough food if it weren't for the moose.

Hares have huge hind feet that act as built-in snowshoes. They crisscross the snow in search of food, and when a new storm comes they are helped rather than harmed. The added snow weights twigs and lowers them still more, and at the same time it deepens the blanket covering the ground. This lifts the hungry animals a few inches higher.

Meadow mice and small rabbitlike rodents called pikas stay active under the snow, their life scarcely slowed down from summer. They feed on grasses and seeds cached weeks earlier. Theirs is a snug world with no cycle of alternating light and dark, and no great rising and falling of temperature. Snow is one of nature's most efficient insulators because the pores between its crystals form countless dead air spaces. When snowshoe hares hop about on the surface at temperatures of −30° F., pikas and meadow mice tunneling beneath a foot or two of snow experience temperatures no lower than 25° or 30° F. above zero. Without snow's blanket these animals would perish. If they stayed at the surface their small bodies would lose life's heat faster than they could rekindle it by constant feeding day and night. Death would come quickly.

Some wildlife, from half-ton bears to 10-pound marmots, hibernate in winter. They sleep away the long months of cold and snow. Body temperatures drop to what would be equivalent to 45° F. for a man (instead of 98°). Their hearts barely beat and their breathing falls to only two or three gentle gasps per minute. The winter reality of the snowshoe hare and the moose mean nothing to them; not even the scrapings of the meadow mice and pikas that share their undersnow realm reach their awareness. The pattern, of course, is worldwide, but Yellowstone offers a unique situation. Each winter, bears there curl up in dens with built-in heating systems. They seek out crevices in the rocky ledges surrounding geyser areas.

Snowshoe hares have large footpads that let them hop about without sinking into the snow.

Wildlife Policies

WHEN YELLOWSTONE FIRST WAS ESTABLISHED AS A NATIONAL park—and for a good many years thereafter—men looked at the wildlife there from their own viewpoint and rated various species according to "usefulness." On an early official park list, golden-eye ducks are mentioned as "not considered a choice bird for eating" and Cassin finches are "a friendly little bird with pleasing color and a rich song." Badgers are "sullen and ugly seeming." Buffalo, elk, and deer were wanted, partly because they had become scarce elsewhere and partly because they were good eating. Wolves, coyotes, mountain lions, and bobcats were not wanted because they preyed on the buffalo, elk, and deer.

On this kind of a basis, park rangers made war against the white pelicans nesting on islands in Yellowstone Lake. The birds catch fish, and men wanted the fish for themselves. For eight years, from 1924 to 1932, eggs were taken from the nests and young pelicans were killed to reduce the size of the colony.

Such a practice is shocking today. In fact, the fish themselves are now protected, with portions of certain lakes and rivers closed to anglers, especially during spawning season. Furthermore, all fishermen are urged to release the trout they catch instead of keeping them. Birds such as ospreys and the pelicans, and mammals such as mink and otters, need fish. They have nowhere else to turn for their food. Man does.

Wildlife policies throughout the world have changed in the century that Yellowstone has been a park. The founding of the park itself was a beginning in America's changed way of thinking about wildlife. Elk and buffalo had nearly disappeared as the frontier was settled and Yellowstone offered a chance to save some of the last great herds. Buffalo had once numbered 60 million. The sound of their running thundered across all of the midcontinent plains, and smaller herds ranged through the mountains to the west as far as eastern Washington and Oregon. East of the Mississippi River, buffalo were native from Hudson Bay to Georgia.

Coyotes—and all wildlife—now are protected in Yellowstone, but this has not always been true.

A traveler, writing in the 1830s, told of the Platte Valley in Nebraska, covered with buffalo as far as he could see, which he estimated as 10 miles ahead and 8 miles from the bluff where he stood to the riverbank. Another early account speaks of a steamer stopped by buffalo in the upper Missouri River and forced to wait for hours while the herd swam across. Trains, too, often were blocked and when this happened, passengers indulged in shooting as many of the beasts as they could, thinking of it as sport though the circumstances were more like slaughter. An Irish lord visiting the West for the purpose of hunting bragged that from 1854 to 1857 he shot 2,000 buffalo, 1,600 elk and deer, and 105 bears. When railroads began to cross the prairies, companies advertized excursions at ten dollars a trip for the purpose of seeing and killing buffalo.

Some of the killing was commercial. The meat of the wild beeves could be marketed and the hides were even more in demand. Beaver fur had become hard to get by 1830 and was going out of style. Buffalo pelts became the mainstay of the fur industry, used to make warm, durable robes. When they lost favor, buffalo leather continued to be valuable. Traders, on the upper Missouri River, offered Indians 3 cups of ground coffee, 6 cups of sugar, or 10 of flour per skin. There are records of 200 robes patiently tanned by Cree women through the winter being traded for 5 gallons of whiskey, and of Crow men accepting necklaces worth sixteen cents in exchange for each robe. Their women thought the pale blue glass beads were wonderful for embroidery, far easier to use than porcupine quills, and more showy.

Nearly 200,000 buffalo hides were shipped from the plains to New Orleans in the peak year of the trade, 1828. As much as forty-five years later, when the peak had long passed, the

Buffalo by the million once grazed the continent, yet without the sanctuary of the park, they might have become extinct.

Wichita, Kansas, newspaper *Eagle* could comment: "It is estimated that there are . . . from one to two thousand men [west of Wichita] shooting buffaloes for their hides alone. . . . An average of two carloads per day, or about a thousand hides per day, for the last two months has been forwarded from Wichita." One hunter claimed that he personally killed over 20,000 buffalo during this period. Another shot almost 6,000 in a single autumn—so many that the continual roar of his rifle left him deaf in his right ear.

By 1884 it was all over. The last shipment of buffalo hides —ever—went out from Dickinson, North Dakota that year, barely over a decade after the park had been established. If it weren't for Yellowstone, wild buffalo probably would have vanished forever. Except for those in the park, about all that remained of the great herds were whitening bones. These were gathered by the wagonload and sold to be ground and used in the manufacture of china and fertilizer. Horns were marketed for knife handles and buttons.

Inside park boundaries, the superintendent estimated in 1898 that only fifty head of buffalo remained. They were mountain buffalo, a type that by habit stay in remote forested country rather than massing on open slopes and valleys as plains buffalo do. For this reason, it may well be that rangers couldn't count them accurately, but in any case, an accurate count or not, officials were worried. They didn't want the population to drop still lower, and to protect against this they decided to bring in buffalo from herds that ranchers in Montana and Texas were trying to domesticate.

These animals were used to breed with the wild herd and gradually numbers built back. The imports were plains buffalo, but the habits of the Yellowstone herd have remained unchanged. They still stay in remote, timbered regions most of the year. In winter, they move to the lower country, sometimes including the snow-free thermal basins, sometimes roaming where the snow lies belly-deep. Biologists estimate that there are 500 buffalo in the park today, probably about half of what were there in the days when Sheep Eater Indians were the sole human residents of Yellowstone.

Buffalo are not the only species that was saved in the Yellowstone area. So were trumpeter swans, the largest species of waterfowl anywhere in the world. These great white birds, nested and fed by the thousands from the Arctic to the Gulf Coast and from the Pacific to the marshes of Indiana and northern Missouri. Then, by 1932 they were down to only a known 69 within all of the United States, although doubtless with other trumpeters, uncounted, in Alaska and Canada. The 69 were discovered at Red Rock Lakes, Montana (just west of Yellowstone) by a biologist working for the National Park

Service. Hot springs keep the lakes from freezing in winter and the area was still remote enough to offer refuge.

During the early 1800s fur companies such as Hudson's Bay handled as many as 2,000 swanskins in a year. For the most part, they were sold in London although American colonists also hunted and used swans. Feathers were made into decorations and writing quills, and the soft inner down was used for powder puffs. Great as the population of swans was, it couldn't stand this pressure, and the species came close to vanishing. Even now that swans no longer are hunted for the market they continue to be killed by shot they accidentally swallow, which causes lead poisoning. Trumpeters stir up the bottom of ponds as they feed, reaching with their long necks and using their bills and also scratching with their webbed feet. The roots of plants are what they're after, but in eating them they also swallow many pellets from shotgun shells. This is true even today, and poisoning is still their major cause of death.

Red Rocks was set aside as a wildlife refuge in 1935. The swans were fed grain and carefully protected, and slowly their numbers began to rebuild. As early as 1938, the Fish and Wildlife Service moved 3 young trumpeters to the elk refuge in Wyoming just south of Yellowstone, and in the following years they planted nucleus populations at other refuges. These transplanted pairs successfully hatched eggs, and gradually swans have returned to much of their former range. Today, an estimated 4,000 or 5,000 trumpeter swans again stretch their wings against the sky. Their wing spans measure up to 10 feet across and flocks move at speeds of 50 miles an hour. See them overhead, or watch a nesting pair swim with their fluffy cygnets, and you can't help but rejoice that trumpeters have been saved. In winter as many as 70 swans at a time have

Trumpeter swans now swim on Yellowstone rivers and lakes, and each spring several pairs nest in the park.

been seen resting and feeding on the Yellowstone River, and each April 10 or 12 pairs nest on ponds scattered through the park.

Among the exhibits at the Smithsonian Institution in Washington, D.C., is one telling the story of extinction. You can see what the Carolina parakeet once looked like, although every one now is dead. You can get an idea about the short-tailed albatross, like a gull the size of a small goose, and about the California condor, believed the actual bird behind Indians' stories of Thunderbird. The great auk is also in the display case, and the Eskimo curlew, the dodo, the passenger pigeon, and others. They all are labeled EXTINCT or NEARLY EXTINCT, according to the actual situation today—all except the trumpeter swan. Its label has been changed to read NOT EXTINCT.

Extinction is a natural process. Judging from the record left by fossils, the average length of time for a species of mammals is about 600,000 years, and for birds a little more than three times that long. The problem is that more and more animals are being directly wiped out by man, not by the normal toll of changes in environment or by competition from similar species. Discussion of wildlife dying out is really discussion of man's activities and attitudes. In the last 400 years 70 or 80 percent of the birds and animals that have become extinct have done so in one way or another at the hand of man.

We shape the landscape to suit ourselves, draining swamps, leveling hills, and straightening rivers. We build cities, tend farms, and raise sheep and cattle. Each year wildlife loses more territory. Each year, too, it is exposed to the poisons we use in agriculture and industry.

Some of the deadly pressure has not been necessary in the past and is not necessary now. The passenger pigeon was hunted until none were left, sometimes to provide meat for the table, more often simply as sport. For centuries the flocks that flew across our eastern states were so great that the sky was darkened by them for an hour at a time. Then they were gone forever, brought down by men's guns.

Snowy egrets nearly were lost from Florida simply because their feathers made fine decorations for women's hats. Crocodiles today are on the brink of dying out because their hides are valuable for shoes and luggage. In the United States 33 species of mammals and 60 species of birds are listed as rare or endangered. National parks offer a last stronghold for some of these species.

Among the animals of Yellowstone, wolves and grizzly bears are the two that are the most seriously threatened in the nation as a whole. Black bears—cousins of grizzlies—are not endangered. Neither are coyotes which, in fact, can adjust so well to changed landscape and the domination of man that they even live inside cities such as Seattle and Los Angeles. Wolves and grizzlies are more shy and also far more feared by man. Exceedingly few are left in the United States, yet Yellowstone is home country for both.

Even in the park, wolves practically disappeared for a time. Partly, this was the result of poisoning and shooting in the early days when such action was seen as protection for the elk. Only in recent years have rangers on back country patrol and hikers again begun to see wolves. Officials think at least 6 now roam the park hinterlands and perhaps as many as a dozen. This is far below the number that were there a century ago, but it seems to be the beginning of a comeback.

Wolves look similar to coyotes but are twice as big, weighing 60 to 100 pounds compared to 20 to 40 pounds for coyotes. Their tracks are 4 or 5 inches long, which is double the size of coyotes' tracks. In the forty-eight United States, northern Minnesota and Michigan are the only areas with wolves other than Yellowstone. In Alaska and across Canada, they still are common. In fact, three or four thousand people visit Algonquin Provincial Park in Ontario each summer and fall to listen to wolves howl. They hear a wild night music that once echoed across the continent but now is rare.

Wolves are not bloodthirsty and vicious, as they are thought to be. They kill to eat but so do all animals that feed on flesh, including ourselves. Sheep from a flock, or domestic cattle, are suitable as a meal, so far as wolves are concerned, and this brought them into conflict with man hundreds of years ago. Furthermore, occasionally wolves become rabid and attack without being provoked, just as dogs with rabies will bite. Man's fear of wolves had this as a basis, and folklore long ago took over from there. When European colonists arrived in America, they battled against wildness in all its forms, including wolves. Nobody bothered to find out what the animals really are like. They just assumed what they had heard was true and did everything possible to rid the land of wolves.

The facts biologists now are learning show no reason for this terror. Wolves, the largest member of the dog family, are also the most shy. They avoid man. Each day finds them searching over a distance of about 45 miles for food, trotting along on their toes instead of on the soles of their feet, thus able to move swiftly and nimbly among rocks and logs. They hunt in packs and feast hugely when they make a kill. They devour as much as 20 pounds apiece, wasting nothing. Wolves return to a carcass until even the hide and hair are gone. They only kill to eat, and they attack weak animals in a herd because they are the easiest to overpower. For the wolves, this is efficiency. For the herd it is a means of staying fit.

The chances of watching—or hearing—a wolf in Yellowstone are still very slight. They are too few and too shy. Bears are more likely to be seen. Both black bears and grizzlies roam the forests, open valleys, and slopes. Perhaps bears, more than any other wildlife, represent man's delight in wildlife and his dilemma. Let a bear stand by the roadside, especially a female with cubs, and cars stop, people gather, and cameras click. Yellowstone has been as loved and publicized for its bears as for its geysers, yet the man-bear relationship has not been a good one. It is unnatural.

By the 1890s, hotels had been built in the park and bears had learned that humans were a good source of food. Their natural diet is anything organic—ants, sedge, grass, roots, the carcass of a moose or elk, and ground squirrels dug out of their burrows. Adding scraps of meat, leftover salad, and jam jars to lick out suited the bears very well. They began to raid hotel garbage dumps and people began to enjoy watching.

Black bears and grizzlies were fed for years, but park policy now calls for leaving them strictly on their own.

Beginning in 1919, regular feeding stations were supplied with garbage each evening and watching the bears eat became as much of a park attraction as looking at Old Faithful or Yellowstone Falls. As many as 30 or 40 bears at a time would gather to paw through the debris, both black bears and grizzlies.

For twenty years this went on. Sows taught their young the routes to the feeding places and generations of bears grew up accepting garbage as the best source of summertime food. The bears were being treated as if they were in a zoo without cages. They had been made into performers in a sideshow, and had lost their natural relation to the land. In 1941 the feeding was stopped, but the bears' hunger and their taste for human food kept on. The stations were closed and the audience gone, but they went on their own to garbage dumps and made nightly rounds of campgrounds to tip over cans and break into campers' supplies. They also begged along the road, accepting sandwiches, potato chips, and candy—and not always paying attention to where the food left off and the fingers began. Bears had lost their fear of humans, and humans had lost their fear of bears. Trouble was inevitable. Probably the only surprise is that there haven't been more injuries.

Bears don't act like lovable Winnie-the-Poohs or Gentle Bens. When a cookie is held out, then teasingly pulled back, they may get angry enough to bite or to cuff with their sharp-clawed, exceedingly powerful paws. When a person comes closer than a bear is willing to permit, it may charge. Every species—man included—is sensitive about being approached too closely. This is especially true when there are young, and a mother bear is sure to charge if a person steps between her and her cubs. A man may not see the cubs, holding onto tree branches overhead or lying in the tall grass, but a bear is sure to see the man. The first case of a bear attack in Yellowstone occurred in 1907. A park visitor chased a grizzly cub and after it ran up a tree kept prodding it with an umbrella. The mother killed the man.

Injuries happen each year to people who ignore the fact that bears are wild and powerful animals, but in spite of human foolishness, and even meanness, the chances of harm from a bear are far below the odds of an automobile wreck, falling while climbing a mountain, or drowning. Statistically, the chances of being hurt by a bear are only one in 1.5 million.

Yet, even aside from the matter of human injury, new wildlife policies have been needed in the relationship between man and bears. A national park isn't intended to be a zoo with animals on exhibit for humans. Bears' taste for human food needed to be broken. Garbage dumps now have been replaced by incinerators and garbage cans have been made so that bears can't get into them. Campers are required to keep groceries in tight containers stored inside their cars, and rangers fine people who offer food to roadside bears.

Certain trails are closed at times when bears, especially grizzlies, need to be in that particular part of the park. This happens when slopes are rich with ripe huckleberries, when white-bark pine nuts are newly fallen from the cones, or when a stream is filled with spawning cutthroat trout. A few campgrounds may be moved away from the main travel route of grizzlies, or may be closed for periods of a few weeks. For example, the Canyon and Fishing Bridge campgrounds are in areas where bears like to dig out roots and a variety of rodents. This takes place early in the season, not long after they have broken hibernation. Later, the bears go elsewhere and people there aren't disruptive to them. The campgrounds then can open.

About 500 black bears and 250 grizzlies live in Yellowstone. The grizzlies are especially valued because they have few havens left. Originally their range reached from the Arctic Circle to Mexico and the Pacific Coast to the Mississippi. The grizzly is the symbol of the California state flag. Yet, in the United States today (outside Alaska), only Yellowstone and Glacier National Park, Montana, harbor sizable populations of grizzly bears. There are also a few in remote corners of Montana, Wyoming, Idaho, and possibly Washington. Alaska and western Canada still have large numbers roaming free, but these have little protection.

Grizzlies, like wolves, avoid man unless they are lured by food. They are huge animals, weighing up to 600 pounds compared to about 300 pounds as a maximum for a black bear. Their shoulders are humped and have a silvery, "grizzled" cast to the fur. Faces are dished and snouts are long. Reared on hind legs, a male grizzly stands 7 or 8 feet high. A black bear seldom reaches more than 5 feet high at the most.

Bears and wolves, and also other predators such as mountain lions, bobcats, and wolverines, have come to be respected and valued by man. The new wildlife policy—the new human attitude—is that in a park as big as Yellowstone there is room enough for all today, as there was in the past. Man's role isn't to overwhelm nature. It is to fit in, to come as a visitor and not as an overlord.

Bobcats, and all forms of wildlife, belong to the park community and are protected within Yellowstone.

Man

AS HUMANS, WE TEND TO THINK OF NATURE IN TERMS OF plants plus insects, animals, birds, and fish—and forget to include ourselves. Yet, we too are part of the overall plan, even though our minds, and now our technology, allow us to dominate. We are not the most abundant species, but our number is growing perhaps too fast and, in any case, we are the most powerful of any species. Much of this is recent.

Journals and paintings from a century and a half ago, give an idea of what Indian life was like when Europeans and Yankees first entered the western plains and mountains, and archaeologists push the story back thousands of years further. They "read" the evidence of stone tools and of animal bones broken open to get out the marrow, and from such evidence they piece together what life must have been like in the days before there were written records.

The only Indians living in Yellowstone when white men first came were the Tukudika, or Sheep Eaters. They built

Indians living in Yellowstone depended so heavily on bighorn sheep that they were called Sheep Eaters.

lodges of poles covered with brush and animal skins. Their diet included elk, deer, and mountain sheep, which they hunted; and there also were berries to gather in the forest and wild onions, camas, and yampa roots to dig. Lakes and rivers provided fish and ducks, and rabbits and squirrels were easy to snare.

Food was available, but that didn't make life comfortable or easy. Yellowstone is high, its winters snowy, cold, and long. The Sheep Eaters lived scattered in small groups or individual families without any of the real tribal organization that was usual where living conditions were better. They had no horses or guns and could not keep pace with the Plains Indians living close by. But they did have two highly valued resources not easy to get elsewhere: obsidian and mountain sheep.

The glassy black obsidian was easy to quarry and to shape into arrowpoints, knives, and scrapers with razor-sharp edges. The sheep were relatively easy to hunt. The Indians followed them into the mountains, shot them, skinned off the hides and cut up the carcasses. Dogs went along to pack out the meat. A pair of poles were tied at one end to a harness fitted across the dogs' shoulders and the other end was allowed to drag. Heavy loads could be lashed to this device, called a *travois*.

Shoshone Indians living south of Yellowstone came into the park to get obsidian and to trade for sheep hides and horn. Sometimes in winter, they came on snowshoes to hunt elk or sheep. It was a long and hard trip but when no meat could be taken in their home country the Shoshones could count on the herds inside Yellowstone's high fastness. Success was practically guaranteed in the thermal basins. There weren't always huge concentrations of animals, but some were sure. Enough to hold off starvation.

Blackfoot Indians raiding out of Canada came south as far as Yellowstone in the early 1800s, attacking Indians and white men alike. Nez Perces with Chief Joseph in charge of women, children, and aged, and others as war chiefs, fled through Yellowstone in 1877. They were escaping from U.S. Army troops that had been sent to settle them onto a reservation in eastern Washington, far from their actual homeland in Oregon. The band had been on the run for months by the time they reached the park area. Near Yellowstone, they came on two prospectors and forced them to go along as guides. They also made hostages of a party of sightseers. Later all were released, badly frightened but unhurt.

In northern Montana, the Nez Perces finally were overtaken by the cavalry, just a few days travel from sanctuary in Canada. They surrendered. Too many had been killed, including women and children, and too many of those who still lived were freezing and starving.

Bannock Indians were another tribe that came into the park

Chief Joseph and a band of Nez Perce Indians fled through Yellowstone soon after it became a park.   The Washington State Historical Society

during this period when changes were taking place, one after another, and the old life of the tribes was about to disappear forever. By 1840 the buffalo no longer could be found on the plains west of Yellowstone, which was Bannock territory. They had been killed by the newly arrived white men and by Indians made more efficient now that they shot rifles and rode horses (which had spread northward from the Spanish settlements in Texas and New Mexico). Without buffalo, the Bannocks had nothing to hunt, yet they refused to accept loss of their life style, which was based on hunting. They wanted meat and hides. They also wanted the excitement of the hunt, for it gave them a chance to show bravery and skill.

Herds still grazed the plains far to the east, and the Bannocks began tortuous yearly journeys across Yellowstone to reach them. Whole families went, a trip of 200 miles that took weeks each way. The poles of the Bannock travoises, drawn by horses, rutted the ground so deeply that the trail through the park still can be followed. Yet, the last trek was made about one hundred years ago, in 1878, six years after Yellowstone had become a park.

Warriors and hunters must have entered Yellowstone to seek guardian spirits, as well as to get meat. A few hot springs may have served as medicinal baths. Obsidian was quarried, and sulfur and ocher (a reddish mineral) were dug for use as paint. Archaeologists have discovered dozens of arrowheads, knives, and other stone tools in the geyser and hot spring basins, some of them lying close to vents.

The remains of fences built of bushes, or low walls of stone, have been found crossing several sagebrush flats. One is several miles long, used to direct the movement of deer to where hunters crouched with their bows and arrows, ready to shoot. Other fences seem to have been corrals that buffalo and maybe also elk were driven into and killed. Bones show butchering marks where stone knives cut them, and archaeologists have found scrapers used in dressing the skins. Bones also have been found at the base of cliffs outside the park— "jumps" that herds were stampeded over. Sometimes this was done by building fires to panic the animals, sometimes by creeping into their midst wrapped in antelope skins as disguise.

Several rings of stones used to hold tepee skins snug against the ground have been found, also charcoal, flakes of stone, and tools. A few stones used for grinding seeds are known in the northern park, and along the shores of Yellowstone Lake someone every now and then finds a stone sinker that once must have been tied to a fishnet.

So far, 224 separate places with evidence of prehistoric Indians have been excavated in the park, and research has only begun. Men evidently arrived in the area eleven or twelve thousand years ago, not long after the glaciers had melted from the land. The climate was colder than now, but gradually it warmed. By about 5000 B.C. it was much warmer than now—a period that scientists refer to as the *altithermal* (*alti* meaning high, and *thermal,* temperature). Great herds of mammoths (elephantlike animals now extinct) and giant buffalo, which were the ancestors of today's buffalo, disappeared from the plains during this period. The change in climate may have destroyed their food supply, or the prehistoric Indians may have hunted them to the point of extermination. Nobody knows.

In any case the cool, green heights of Yellowstone became attractive and men shifted there to hunt deer and elk and to fish. For about four thousand years the climate stayed hot, then it cooled and became about the same as it is today. Buffalo and elk again roamed the low country outside Yellow-

The first white men to enter the cool green heights of Yellowstone were trappers in search of beaver.

Leonard Lee Rue III

stone and men began moving back. Indian life started to form in much the same patterns as reported by the early explorers and trappers entering the northern plains.

Fur trappers were the first white men to enter Yellowstone. John Colter, who was with Lewis and Clark in 1805, asked permission to leave the expedition on its homeward journey and head into Yellowstone to spend the winter trapping. He was the first of many, for, as the rest of the West became trapped out, the remote, high reaches of Yellowstone remained rich in wildlife.

The trappers lived off the land as closely as the Indians did. They traveled widely, counted on success at hunting to provide food, endured heat and cold and discomfort. Their number never was more than a few hundred and, except for the annual rendezvous where furs were traded, they lived far scattered and always on the move. Yet their effect was enormous. They did more than take their own living from the land, and in this they differed from the Indians. The trappers, or "mountain men" as they were called, gathered the resources of the land and shipped them out.

Osborne Russell, who trapped the Yellowstone country in the 1830s, wrote about trading with Sheep Eater Indians for hides: "We get a large number of elk, deer, and sheep skins from them of the finest quality and three large panther skins (mountain lion) in return for awls, axes, kettles, tobacco, ammunition, etc. They would throw the skins at our feet and say, 'Give us whatever you please for them and we are satisfied. We can get plenty of skins . . .' "

Beaver were especially sought. The equipment for taking them was nothing more than a bottle of bait, half a dozen traps, and a knife. The traps were set in shallow water and chained in place so they couldn't be pulled up onto the bank. The bait was a musky oil. Beaver would come to sniff sticks that had been dipped in the musk and set upright beside the traps. As their nose touched the bait, they were caught, and they soon drowned. Their skins were stretched on wooden frames, dried, folded, and packed into 100-pound bales.

Trappers, and the Indians working for them, took every beaver possible. When animals were wiped out in one area, the men moved to another. By Russell's time beaver had disappeared in much of the West. Their fur was in particular demand for men's hats and if it hadn't been for the growing popularity of high silk hats the animals might have been completely killed off.

Most mountain men had little education. They told stories of what they saw, but few could write about their experiences. Some of what Colter reported was included in the official account of the Lewis and Clark expedition. From it, and from stories that made the rounds by word of mouth, the public began to wonder about Yellowstone. It seemed a strange corner of "Louisiana," as all of the territory newly purchased from France was called. Osborne Russell's diary, and those of one or two other trappers who could write, gave the first detailed record of what the land and the life were like (although they were not widely read at the time).

"Near where we encamped were several hot springs which boil perpetually," Russell wrote of Yellowstone. "Near these was an opening in the ground about eight inches in diameter from which hot steam issues continually with a noise similar to that made by the steam issuing from the safety valve of an engine." He added that it could be heard for five or six miles.

In another passage he wrote of finding about fifty springs of boiling water that one of his companions had visited the year before. "He [the friend] wanted to show us some curiosities," Osborne noted. "The first spring we visited was about ten feet in diameter and threw up mud with a noise similar to boiling soup." This must have been a mud pot.

Other springs, which they camped near later on, Osborne says would "slowly boil for an hour and then shoot forth." These were geysers in the Old Faithful area.

Today, we come on such sights with advance knowledge of what to expect, but they were almost beyond belief for men discovering them for the first time. However, surprise didn't stop them from putting the hot water to use. Osborne tells that it was "very serviceable to the hunter in preparing his dinner when hungry for here his kettle is always ready and boiling." His system was to tie meat with a cord, lower it into a hot spring, then pull it out. No camping place except in Yellowstone offered the mountain men such convenience.

Next to enter the region, after the fur brigades, were prospectors in search of gold. They made enough strikes so that by 1860, men hungry for riches were sweeping through the mountains on their way to boom towns in Montana. As they traveled, they looked everywhere for additional promise of ore, and one of the first maps of Yellowstone drawn by Walter W. deLacy comes from this period. He was an engineer who found no sign of gold, but made detailed notes of the topography.

More and more people were hearing about Yellowstone and starting to wonder about it for its own sake, not just for what fur or gold it might yield. In the late 1860s two exploring parties saddled their horses and rode into Yellowstone. One made only a short trip and wrote no report. The other spent a month and on return wrote an account that was sent to the *New York Tribune*, *Scribner's* magazine, and *Harper's* magazine. The editors of each turned the story down. They couldn't believe that such a land of boiling, spouting water was real.

The National Park

ONCE MEN DECIDED TO TAKE A CAREFUL LOOK AT YELLOW-
stone, events built quickly toward knowledge and recognition
of the area that today is the park. In 1870, a third party of
explorers rode into Yellowstone, this one a large and official
group headed by Henry D. Washburn, the surveyor general of
Montana Territory, and with military escort under the leader-
ship of Lieutenant Gustavus C. Doane. The next year, Congress voted funds to send a team of Geological Survey scientists into Yellowstone to make a thorough investigation, and
settle the question of whether stories about it were true or false.
Ferdinand V. Hayden, a geologist, headed the undertaking.
With him were experts in the study of everything from plants,
animals, and insects to minerals and weather.

The men on the 1870 exploring trip had been excited by
what they found, and it was their enthusiasm that started the
process of making Yellowstone a national park. The area
seemed so unusual and beautiful to them that they felt it

The first official survey of Yellowstone was made by the Hayden Expedition in 1871. Ferdinand Hayden, head of the expedition, is shown seated by his tent in the top picture.   National Park Service

should be kept natural forever and should belong to the whole nation rather than to private owners. Nathaniel P. Langford, a member of the expedition and a man influential in politics, took the lead in urging that the area be set aside as a park. He wrote articles and traveled through the East, lecturing about the wonders he and his party had seen. It was at one of these lectures that Hayden became impressed enough to recommend the full scientific investigation, which he led in the summer of 1871.

On his return to Washington, D.C., Hayden's reports prompted Congress to act, and on March 1, 1872 President Ulysses S. Grant signed a bill making Yellowstone a national park, the first in the world. Never before, anywhere, had public land been set aside by law for the purpose of staying forever wild and accessible to everyone who wanted to come and see for himself. Wealthy nobles in Europe and Asia had owned hunting preserves, but the land was private, open only to them. Yellowstone was to be owned by the public, and it was intended for public use.

How to manage the new park became the question. There weren't any others like it, so there was no example to follow. Also, Congress had not provided any money. They agreed with the idea of a park, but weren't practical about how it could be cared for. Poachers were shooting elk and buffalo, and also setting fires to drive herds out of the park onto land where they could be slaughtered without violating any law. Buffalo heads were worth as much as $500 to $1,500 as trophies and few areas had buffalo left. Elk sold well as meat.

Visitors who had come to enjoy the park were damaging it by writing their names on geyser cones and hot spring terraces, and even breaking rock formations to take home as souvenirs. "The visitors prowled about with shovel and ax, chopping and hacking and prying up great pieces of the most ornamental work they could find; women and men alike joining in the barbarous pastime," reads a despairing report of the first superintendent.

"Tourists as a rule continue to test the power of the geysers by throwing timber in them," reads another report. "This, and the neglect of many campers to extinguish their fires, gives me all I can do."

By 1886, fourteen years after Yellowstone had become a park, Congress put the Army in charge of it. There was no National Park Service at the time and the superintendents had never been given proper money or authority to work with. Soldiers were sent to half a dozen posts dotted through the 2-million-acre wilderness of the park and from there they patrolled on horseback and on skis. They had little real authority, but they could order poachers and others who were abusing the land to leave the park. This they did—by seeing to it that the men walked to the farthest boundary, not the closest. It could mean a hike of hundreds of miles for the offenders, depending on where they happened to be when the soldiers found them.

Soldiers patrolled the park on horseback in summer and on skis in winter during the years that the Army had charge of Yellowstone. National Park Service

The first travel through the park was by horse-drawn carriage, here shown leaving the inn at Mammoth Hot Springs. **National Park Service**

The system worked. Poachers were discouraged.

The Army was so admired for its effectiveness that in 1891, it was given responsibility for Yosemite, Sequoia, and General Grant parks, which had been established in the High Sierra Mountains of California. Germany, Japan, and several states in the United States asked the Army for information on how to manage parks, and a professor at Harvard suggested that all the nation's forests should be put under Army care with forestry taught at West Point. However, the Army felt its prime responsibilities lay elsewhere and, in 1916, Congress established the National Park Service to take over administration of the parks.

Forty-four years had passed since Yellowstone had become a park. Roads had been built to ease sightseeing, and stagecoaches drawn by from four to six horses, carried tourist parties around the park with overnight accommodations at hotels.

Roads were either dusty or badly rutted and muddy in the early days of automobile travel.

The roads were dusty. One traveler complained that anybody who "would permit women and children to enter the park, with the roads in the present condition, is an old scoundrel."

Automobiles began coming in 1915. Regulations limited their speed to 12 miles per hour going uphill, 10 going downhill, and 8 when approaching a curve. The pace was modest, but it ushered in the present era of summer visitors thronging to taste wilderness and to see the special wonders of Yellowstone.

At the time the park was established, the Congressional act setting aside the land stated that it was "reserved and withdrawn from settlement, occupancy, or sale . . . and set aside as a public park or pleasuring ground for the benefit and enjoyment of the people." That was in 1872.

Congress had debated the idea of a park and decided in favor of it largely because Hayden assured them the region was worthless for mining, logging, or grazing. Money was not to be made from such land, the argument went, so nothing would be lost by making it a national park. It was useless for civilization. Wild land had no value. Worth came only from using it.

Colonists arriving in America from Europe found nothing to cherish about the wildness of the coast they had come to; their hopes were pinned on gaining control of nature. The attitude reaches far back. The Old Testament mentions the word "wilderness" 240 times, always as a wasteland and completely undesirable, never with a sense of beauty or joy. At best, wild country was a place where a man could test himself spiritually.

Even farther back in our cultural heritage the ancient Greeks believed that an evil being half goat, half man lived in the forest and among the wild peaks. From his name, *Pan,* comes the word "panic." People were afraid to enter his domain.

Other cultures have not viewed nature this way. The Shinto religion of Japan saw the mountains, the forests, the storms as gods. In India, Hinduism taught that man is a part of nature, not set in opposition with a need to conquer it. In America, Indian tribes lived closely with the land, aware that they depended on it for food and raw materials. They hunted and harvested, and were subservient to the seasons. Fire was about the only tool they had for altering the environment to better suit their needs, and they used it widely. Indian people didn't romanticize nature, but they respected it and tried to stay in harmony with it. They had to. Otherwise they couldn't live.

Romanticism began in the cities of Europe and New England in the 1800s. Industrialization was new. Men limited to planting fields and herding stock had changed the land, but almost always in pleasing ways. Not so with industrialization. Ugliness crept into villages and workers began spending long hours toiling indoors. Along with this came a feeling that nature and the outdoor life were good. Poets, philosophers, and artists turned their talents to praising forests, mountains, and rivers.

This feeling has grown as remaining wild land has shrunk, and there also has come a slow rekindling of the sort of awareness the Indians had. All species, humans included, belong to nature. Through technology, we thought for a time that we had separated ourselves from the environment. Now, we know that we were wrong. National parks and other wild lands are giving scientists a chance to study relationships that developed hundreds of thousands of years ago.

Yellowstone, today is valued as a sample of pristine America. It is untouched nature to be enjoyed, safeguarded, and passed on to the future.

Park lands remain largely wilderness—"home" for wildlife such as these nesting great-blue herons.   **National Park Service**

Travel Guide

Summer. Most people visit Yellowstone sometime between May and September or early October. Days generally are sunny during these months, with maximum temperatures around 80° F. and occasionally approaching 100° F. during July and August. Thunderstorms are common. Occasionally, there may be flurries of snow. Nighttime temperatures, even in midsummer, often put a skim of ice on rain puddles, and they are sure to make park visitors reach for warm sweaters.

Winter travel. Temperatures in winter can be bitterly cold. Snow may fall for days at a time and winds rampage—or there may be sunshine and a feeling of warmth despite thermometer readings of –30 or –40° F. Snow generally builds from 2 to 6 feet deep. Yellowstone Lake freezes over; most rivers do not. Only the north road into the park is kept open for automobiles. Snowmobile trips to Old Faithful are offered, and private snowmobiles are allowed on all roads (but not allowed to travel cross-country). There are no ski facilities in the park, but ski touring is splendid for those who are equipped and experienced; it is not recommended for beginners because of the wilderness terrain, and the likelihood of severe weather and prolonged storms.

Accommodations. Campgrounds are available both in the park and outside its boundaries, year-round. A concessionaire operates hotels and cabin resorts, with some rooms available even in winter. Motels can be found next to the park in West Yellowstone and Gardiner, Wyoming and Cooke City, Montana.

Meals and Groceries. Restaurants and coffee shops are at Canyon, Fishing Bridge, Lake, Mammoth, Old Faithful, Roosevelt, and West Thumb. The same locations, plus Tower Falls, have stores that sell groceries, film, souvenirs, and fishing tackle. The store and dining room at Mammoth stay open all year.

Roads. Five paved roads in Wyoming and Montana enter Yellowstone and a gravel road wanders into the southwest corner from Idaho (but does not connect with the rest of the road system). The Cooke City–Red Lodge road entering from the northeast is one of the most splendid mountain drives in the West, offering views of high peaks in the distance and snowbanks close at hand even in late July.

Inside the park, 300 miles of road lead to points of interest. Some are quiet one-way drives intended for leisurely enjoyment. You can sample the Old Gardiner Road, near park headquarters, which leads down a mountainside and across a sagebrush flat where mule deer and antelope by the dozen are likely to be seen. Or you can drive the Fountain Flat Road

Trails thread the back country far beyond the sight of roads and the sound of human crowds.   Bob and Ira Spring

along the Firehole River watching for elk and Canada geese; the Blacktail Plateau or Bunsen Peak roads, which flame with golden aspen each autumn, or the Firehole Canyon and Virginia Cascades roads, following the winding courses of rivers and crossing through lodgepole pine forest.

Some national parks are now providing sightseeing buses and free shuttle buses as replacements for private automobiles. The programs are experimental and change from time to time. Check the current status for Yellowstone.

Trails. Lakes, waterfalls, thermal basins, mountain peaks, and emerald meadows all lie beyond the roadways, reached on foot or on horseback. In the back country you can escape the crowds of sightseers and find the same wilderness that the Indians and the first explorers knew. Check with park rangers before starting out for an overnight hike. Be sure to carry maps and a compass (and know how to use them), rain gear, sunburn protection, and warm sleeping bags.

For short hikes, join one of the naturalist-led walks. These are open to all, lasting from an hour or two to a full day, everybody carrying their own lunch. Printed schedules and destinations are posted at ranger stations and museums. Nature trails with leaflets to guide you from feature to feature are located at several of the thermal basins. They are short, pleasant, and give a deepened understanding of the forces that have shaped the park and continue to make it special.

There also are trails to sample on your own for an hour or two, or a day. Try the hike to Mystic Falls beyond Biscuit Basin, or to Wraith Falls east of Mammoth. Walk across the sage hummocks in the Lamar Valley looking for pothole lakes where ducks paddle, and coyotes come to drink and hunt. Or go to Artists Paint Pots near Norris for a small, colorful, out-of-the-way thermal basin. Be sure to walk to the bluff above Old Faithful, to stroll the terraces of Mammoth Hot Springs, and to hike to the bottom of the Lower Falls of the Yellowstone (if you are energetic; it's a 1,000-foot drop, descending by walkways and stairs that are sprayed with mist from the waterfall).

Boating. Powerboats and rowboats are available for rent at Grant Village and Bridge Bay on Yellowstone Lake. If you have your own boat, you'll find launch ramps at these two locations and also near Steamboat Point and on Lewis Lake.

The South and Southeast arms of Yellowstone Lake are open only to hand-propelled craft such as canoes and kayaks. The same is true of Shoshone Lake, 10 miles long, reached in half a day by paddling across Lewis Lake and then paddling

The Southeast Arm of Yellowstone Lake rewards canoeists with scenery and a chance to watch wildlife.   *Bob and Ira Spring*

and lining your canoe up the 3-mile Lewis River into Shoshone Lake. For a trip to upper Yellowstone Lake, allow at least a week. It is a long paddle from the nearest launch point to the southern arms. However, the rewards are almost sure: chances to watch moose feeding in marshes, see ducks and mergansers shepherding their downy young, and ospreys plunging from sky to lake after fish.

Be sure to check on current boating regulations whether planning a short trip or a long camping excursion. All boats must have permits, obtainable at ranger stations.

Fishing. Seven species of fish are taken by anglers in the park (cutthroat, grayling, whitefish, rainbow, brown trout, lake trout, and brook trout). Seasons and limits are set to suit the best interests of the fish and the birds and mammals that depend on them for food, not necessarily to suit the pleasure of man. Ask about current regulations.

Thermal Basins. The largest geyser basins are located in the western park, easily accessible by road. Information on eruptions is available at visitor centers, including charts that list the time of the most recent eruptions and the predictions of the next ones. (Predictions are just that, however: predictions. What actually happens may or may not be the same as human expectations.)

Mammoth Hot Springs is the largest hot-spring terrace in the world, gushing forth 700,000 gallons of water daily and bringing tons of dissolved minerals to the surface. Roaring Mountain is a hillside with dozens of hissing steam vents and a small, hot lake. Norris Geyser Basin ranks as the hottest and the most active thermal area in the park. Fountain Paint Pot is perhaps the largest mud pot, and lying beyond it is one of the most interesting thermal basins, with steam vents, geysers, and a hot spring that has colorful runoff channels. Old Faithful is one of several showy geysers in the Upper Basin, including Grand and Giant, which each shoot higher than Old Faithful (although nowhere near so regularly).

WARNING. Do not leave the boardwalks and trails that lead through the thermal basins. Stepping off is dangerous because crusts may break, dropping you into pockets of steam or scalding water.

Wildlife. MacMinn Bench, near park headquarters, is one of the best places to watch for bighorn sheep, especially in spring and fall. Mule deer are certain there, too, and elk and antelope are probable. (This is a hike, requiring at least two or three hours. Be sure to carry binoculars, also water if the day is hot.)

Buffalo are most easily seen in winter. They tend to move into high country in summer as soon as the snow has melted

Old Faithful, symbol of Yellowstone, has erupted about every hour for years. Other geysers are less predictable.

enough to let them find grazing. Hayden Valley and Lamar Valley are good places to look in fall and late spring, as well as in winter.

Bull elk set the air to ringing with the sound of their bugling and the crack of their antlers as they battle for control of the females each September and October. Coyotes sometimes can be found checking around the edge of a herd, or trotting across sagebrush flats, nose to the ground, searching for mice and squirrels.

Black bears are widely distributed and may be happened upon in almost any meadow, sagebrush flat, or forested hillside. Hayden Valley is perhaps the best place to look for grizzlies from your car. They often feed there on the grassy, distant hillsides. (WARNING: Never try to approach a bear, or any of the park's other large animals. They may think you intend to harm them and charge. Females with young are especially dangerous. When hiking, keep up steady talking or tie a bell, or a can with pebbles inside it, to your belt or pack. This will warn grizzlies of your approach and let them run off before they feel threatened.)

Yellowstone Lake is the largest mountain lake in the 50 States. A road parallels part of its shore; part is reached only by trail.

Wildlife as large and powerful as a bull moose and as small and vulnerable as a golden eye duckling typify Yellowstone wildlife.

Moose tend to stay in willow thickets, along quiet rivers and lakeshores, and in marshy meadows. Or you may come on one at the edge of the forest, perhaps even having it walk through your camp at night.

Birds are everywhere in the park. Ospreys can be seen along the Yellowstone River, hovering overhead, plunging to the water to catch fish, or sitting in trees. Trumpeter swans may be found in any lake or along quiet stretches of rivers. Ducks and geese are common. In spring, sandhill cranes court and trumpet their wild music from the meadows between Mammoth and Norris, and beside the Yellowstone River.

Information. For up-to-date information on park regulations, seasons, and travel opportunities, or to purchase booklets and maps, write The Superintendent, Yellowstone National Park, Wyoming 82190.

Index

Italics indicate a photograph on a page not otherwise indexed.